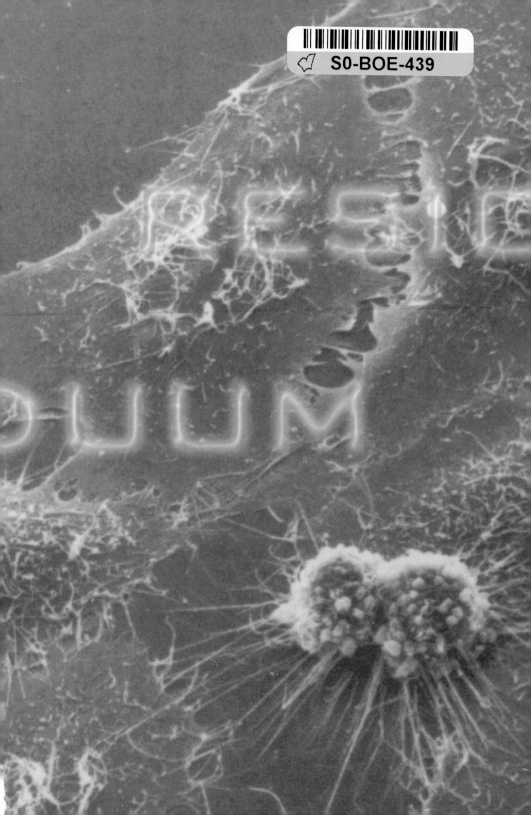

CLEVELAND STATE UNIVERSITY POETRY CENTER
RECENT TITLES

The Hartford Book by Samuel Amadon

Rust or Go Missing by Lily Brown

The Grief Performance by Emily Kendal Frey

Stop Wanting by Lizzie Harris

Vow by Rebecca Hazelton

The Tulip-Flame by Chloe Honum

Render / An Apocalypse by Rebecca Gayle Howell

A Boot's a Boot by Lesle Lewis

Say So by Dora Malech

50 Water Dreams by Siwar Masannat

Mule by Shane McCrae

Festival by Broc Rossell

The Firestorm by Zach Savich

Mother Was a Tragic Girl by Sandra Simonds

I Live in a Hut by S.E. Smith

I Burned at the Feast: Selected Poems of Arseny Tarkovsky
translated by Philip Metres and Dimitri Psurtsev

Bottle the Bottles the Bottles the Bottles by Lee Upton

Adventures in the Lost Interiors of America by William D. Waltz

Uncanny Valley by Jon Woodward

You Are Not Dead by Wendy Xu

For a complete list of titles please visit
WWW.CSUPOETRYCENTER.COM

RESIDUUM

MARTIN ROCK

Cleveland State University Poetry Center
Cleveland, Ohio

ISBN 978-0-9963167-2-9

First Edition

19 18 17 16 15   5 4 3 2 1

This book is published by the Cleveland State University Poetry Center,
2121 Euclid Avenue, Cleveland, Ohio 44115-2214
www.csupoetrycenter.com and is distributed by
SPD / Small Press Distribution, Inc. WWW.SPDBOOKS.ORG.

Cover image: Bedelgeuse, *Wellness*, digitally composed anatomical collage.
© Travis Bedel. Printed with permission from the artist.

Residuum was designed and typeset by Martin Rock in Baskerville & Bank Gothic.

LIBRARY OF CONGRESS CATALOGING IN PUBLICATION DATA

Names: Rock, Martin, author.
Title: Residuum / Martin Rock.
Description: Cleveland, Ohio : Cleveland State University Poetry Center, [2016]
Identifiers: LCCN 2015051340 | ISBN 9780996316729 (softcover)
Classification: LCC PS3618.O35435 A6 2016 | DDC 811/.6--dc23

FOR MY WIFE, HEATHER

& IN MEMORY OF TOM JUNGERBERG

Since the word is inaccurate, it is crossed out.
Since it is necessary, it is left legible.

MARTIN HEIDEGGER

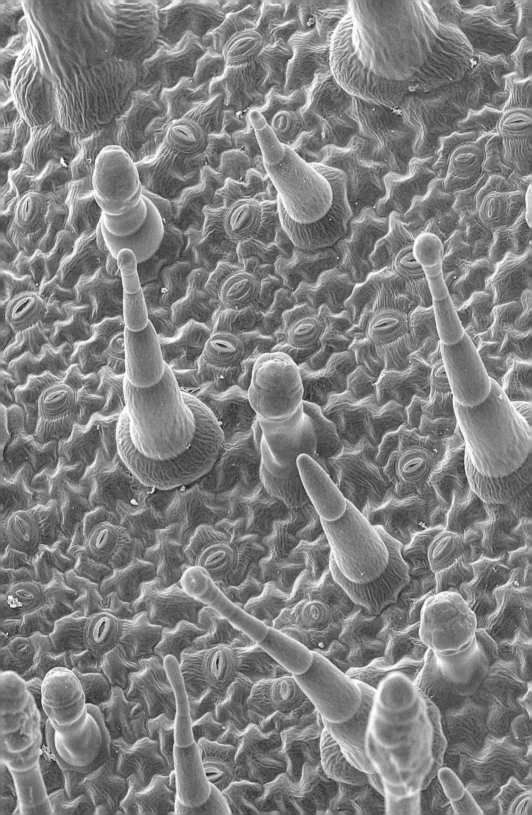

I could find you amongst a pile of ~~leaves~~
                              sleeping animals

& in ~~the squalor of the overhanging vines~~
     the shade of the hole in ~~the sun~~
                         your head

could put my finger through & thrust

& ~~parry~~
   plummet like ~~a buttress into the sea~~
                 swallowed fish into ~~stomach acid~~
                               the ~~desert~~
                                   city of tents in the desert

So ~~I said I am Ezra~~ I did not say
~~Every time the bucks went clattering~~ I did not say

      ~~I did not say~~ the thing you heard

            The particulate matter of ~~breath~~
                           ~~words spoken into a well~~
                    a lithe & well-wrought prayer

remains ~~like chemical residue~~ inside one's genetic material

                and opens itself to ~~revision~~
                    mutation

There is ~~no greed~~
      this fear before the ~~furlough~~
            extradition

         of a ~~body~~
           corpse into the ~~copse~~
              ~~funeral pyre~~
              unnecessarily expensive box

& rend my flesh & feed my fingers
     like ~~stickpin worms to crows~~
         chicken wings to ~~round-faced children~~
            ~~government officials~~
            television pundits who talk & talk

        The connective material is ~~evident in speech~~
              ~~but~~ invisible ~~on the page~~

I should be ~~in the jungle~~
         ~~taking shots~~
            kneeling at the feet of a ~~holy-man~~
                  woman

   with tremendous ~~breasts~~
         capacity for ~~love~~
            leadership

who wears an expression of ~~biological and political revisionism~~
       immense

      & unfocused tenderness

*You must read between the line*s I've been told
      but never *You must read through them*
         never *The lines are interdimensional sutures*

   Entire ~~words~~
     worlds are ~~deleted~~
       ~~marked for deletion~~
       left in the sun to become

          the spongiform of distant planets

    Never *The thing you ~~don't~~ see is the thing that claims you*

This is ~~constitutional and civil~~ engagement
This is ~~the~~ twinned syntax ~~and semantics of DNA~~
This is speaking ~~from a position of surplus privilege~~
This is ~~erasure of~~ the voices that cannot be ~~erased~~
This is ~~my stand against~~ the binary

I've worn ~~out~~ each ~~argument~~
        invisible thread like ~~a suit~~
              a snake wears its skin

    & then have sloughed it off again

The ~~language of bacteria and viruses~~
   burbles and clicks inside my own stomach

     know ~~what it is to become remains~~
       ~~the explosion and what is fused~~
       ~~the chemical film inside my mouth & throat~~
       the movement of the unseen hand

~~Objects are smaller than they appear~~ it does not say

    This is ~~not~~ an act of ~~erasure~~
        resistance

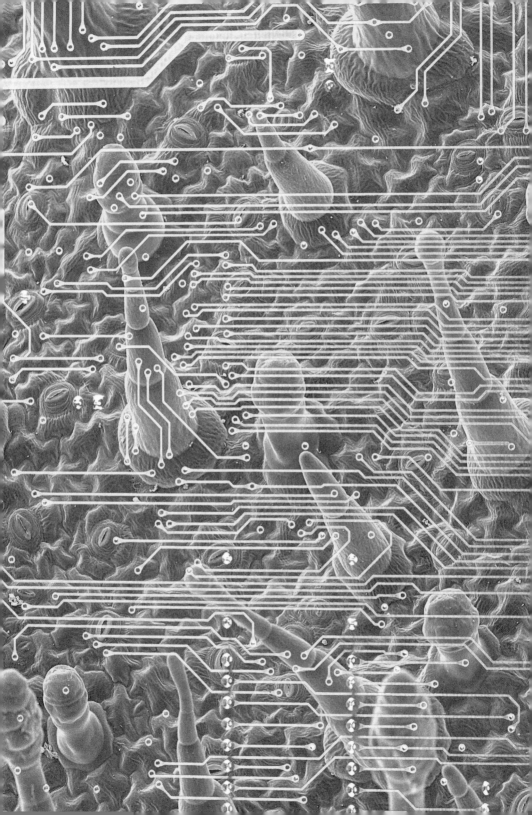

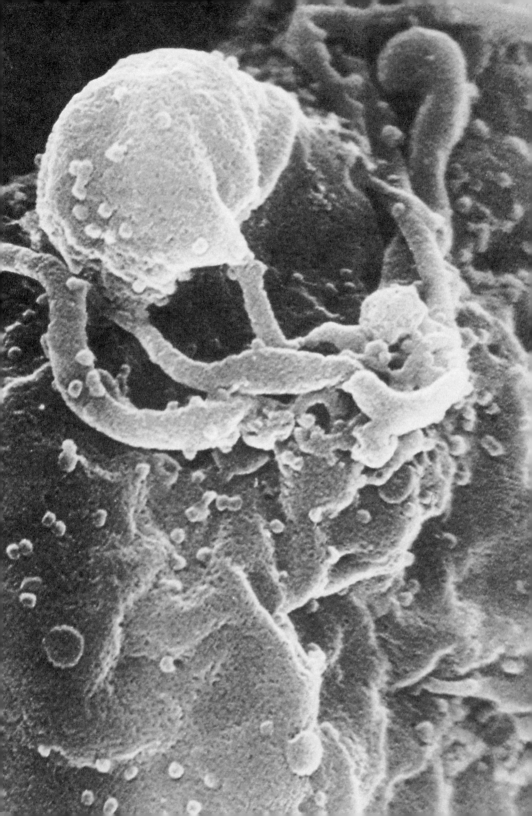

What moth distracts the ~~seamstress from her needlework~~
                           soldier from her ~~art~~
                                    trade of ~~killing~~
                                             distantly dropping

objects that are felt ~~before they're seen~~
                    ~~as one feels and does not feel one's own eventual death~~
                    in the sand

                    as billowing wind

    A bomb ~~is but a fleck of ash in the blasted sky before it lands~~
            does not exist inside ~~these dusty pockets~~
                                   ~~this worn-out body~~
                                   the great American supermarket

            where I buy ~~blackberries~~
                        ~~plums~~
                        plastic bags of apples

            Of this ~~I can be certain~~
                    I am American

❧

~~I want to prick my thumb on thorns~~
~~I want to bleed on fruit~~
I want to earn a place in the world of form

❧

There is a war ~~to claim the hearts & minds~~
                    inside our bodies playing out

Humans are mostly ~~in~~human

The organisms that grow inside us ~~escape when we are dead~~
                                    ~~die when we die~~
                                    outnumber even the billions

of children that will ~~be born in the next ten years~~
                        learn to ~~disguise themselves as insects in video games~~
                        fashion & bargain & populate

                        while inside their guts tens of thousands of
nonhuman bacteria go about the business of how to filter out the poison
they've consumed

❧

I've grown terrified of ~~antibiotics~~
                        ~~pre-packaged food~~
                        ~~video screens in stadiums~~
                        ~~electricity spilling from an unlit street~~
                        ~~the vague & lasting threat of terrorism~~
                        ~~strangers entering and exiting movie theaters~~
                        ~~an iota of unknown breath on my arm~~
                        ~~policemen & their guns~~
                        ~~the invisible economy that breathes~~
                        the hypnotic directives of pop music

❧

If language is twinned as DNA our ~~tongues are forked~~
~~healers~~
doctors must learn

to speak in metaphors of ~~war~~
annhililation

I attack the enemy within by ~~*means of cathartics and refrigerants*~~
releasing him of the status of enemy

& when he is ~~no longer~~ my enemy

I acknowledge his gifts

❧

The viruses are ~~most ornate & pleasing to the eye~~
shaped like ~~planetary bodies~~
~~Gordian knots~~
~~globes of pollen~~
degree-zero Koosh balls

They ~~congregate as boils~~
~~float through the body like nautical mines~~
appear in black & white images

as alien & impenetrable life forms

hell-bent on human death

~~& I cannot distinguish them from nothingness~~

~~A mind is an impossible thing to waste~~
~~Human intelligence is not the only intelligence~~
Slime molds solve mazes by becoming the shape of the maze

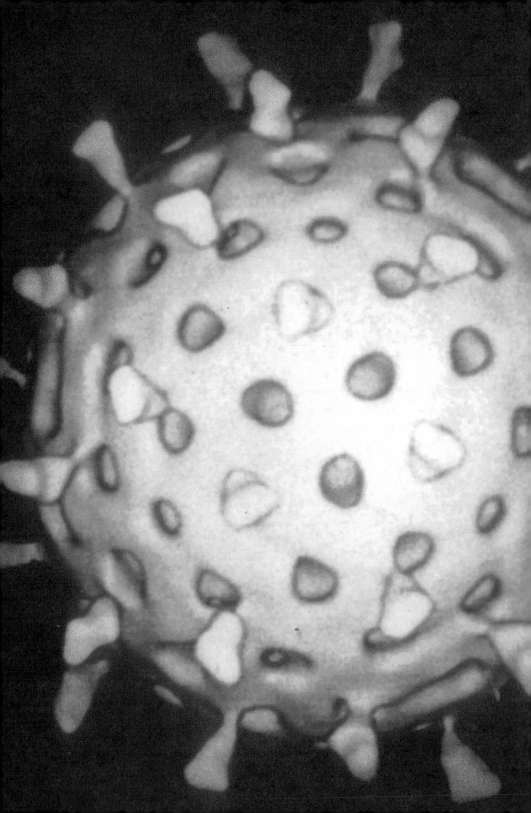

For you my ~~unsentimental~~ bee the race ~~is ending~~

                to the honey pot

culminates in thousands of ~~species dying~~

          jobs for ~~child~~ laborers

     with ~~adorably~~ tiny paintbrushes

          to pollenate the blossoms of ~~star apples~~

                    ~~bucket orchids~~

                    ~~okra~~

                    ~~cashews~~

                    ~~blackberries~~

                    ~~plums~~

                    ~~chili peppers~~

                    ~~buckwheat~~

                    ~~guava~~

                    ~~cocoa~~

                    ~~watermelons~~

                    ~~jack beans~~

                    ~~horse beans~~

                    ~~sword beans~~

                    ~~crownvetch~~

                    ~~durian~~

                    ~~loquats~~

                    ~~feijoa~~

                    Kola nuts

❧

Everyone's ~~grandparents~~
                ~~great-grandparents~~
                ancestors at one point ~~were inculcated with magic~~
                                ~~have tasted nepenthe~~
                                ~~drank potions of forgetfulness~~
                                ~~could converse with plants~~
                                ~~were quantum physicists~~
                                ~~were molecular biologists~~
                                ~~worked on oil rigs~~
                                contracted the ~~white man's~~ illness

                                of ~~syphilis~~
                                        ~~alcoholism~~
                                        pleonexia

& ~~bought & bought~~
   dreamt of buying ~~Cadillacs~~
                                ~~women~~
                                ~~horses~~
                grain to feed their ~~families~~
                                        ~~children~~
                                        spirits that were lost

❧

& those who would choose to ~~return to the plants~~
                                ~~buy back their rivers~~
                                drink the putrid brew

                ~~would vomit & shit onto the ground~~

are ~~poisoned~~
     ~~filled with soot~~
     cleansed of the ~~tapeworm~~
                        hole in their throats these hungry ghosts

22

Of course we die every moment I have ~~killed you~~
                                ~~been killed by you~~
                                been delivered

as an earworm in the course of your ~~daily chores~~
                                ~~nostalgia for childhood~~
                                endless stream of implausable sexts

            As you read this I am ~~dead again &~~ born

into the river I vomit & shit I am a ~~cannibal~~
                                product of ~~the West~~
                                          ~~the earth~~
                                DNA's need to ~~self-replicate~~
                                                create

            new permutations of life
                                through mutation

            In the woods I found a ~~den of foxes~~
                                fungus on the forest floor

            It locked ~~eyes with me~~
                                its elements within my own network of neurons

            & both transformed

~~It was~~ the ~~thought of her~~ brain ~~that~~ assumed the ~~shape of a~~ phantom

                                it did ~~not~~ say

It is a joy to admit I was born!

& yes I have ~~felt so proud to get at the meaning of poems~~
    lost my cognizance again at the ~~edge of the forest~~
        ~~bubonic symphony~~
        ~~rock hall of famine~~
        ~~rave in Miami~~
        mall listening to Jay Z

I was attempting to decipher

the significance of the lyric I have reckoned much I
have practiced I have been open to the breathing of animals

    & to you supercomputer you carpenter who has
put up four houses this month & you prisoner asleep in your cell you
permaculturist you trader who breathes at the mouth of the terrifying
prism of economy & you merchant you hog-butcher you swarm of ants
you coder at work on the future languages of noncorporeality you dreamer
you pilot you terraform farmer you ambush of tigers you gam of whales
& you tiny breathing machine you on the oil derricks you ecowarrior
& activist you artist & fisherman you brother you army of caterpillars
you dealer of cards & bodies you security guard asleep in your car &
you bed of clams you bask of crocodiles you judge you pomegranate
you magnate you picker of noses & fruit you gerrymanderer you electric
razor you fry of eels you bloat of hippos you addict you lawyer & doctor
& mothers you fathers you brothers you sisters you readers you gods

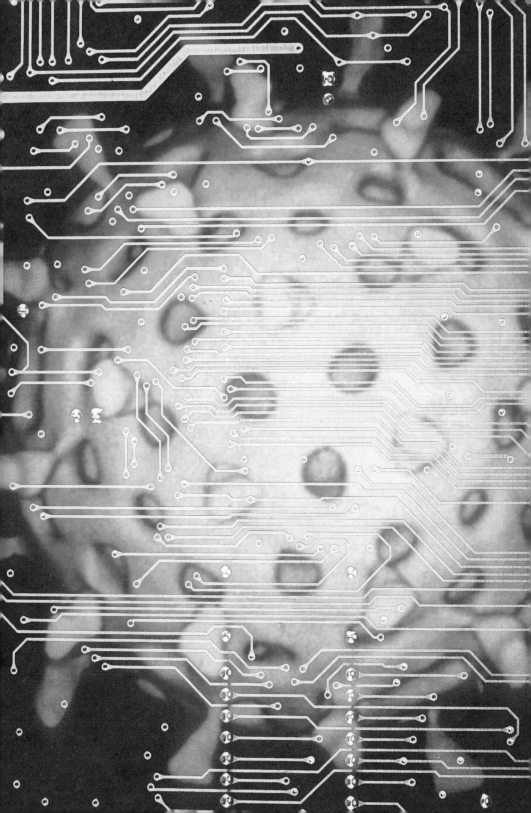

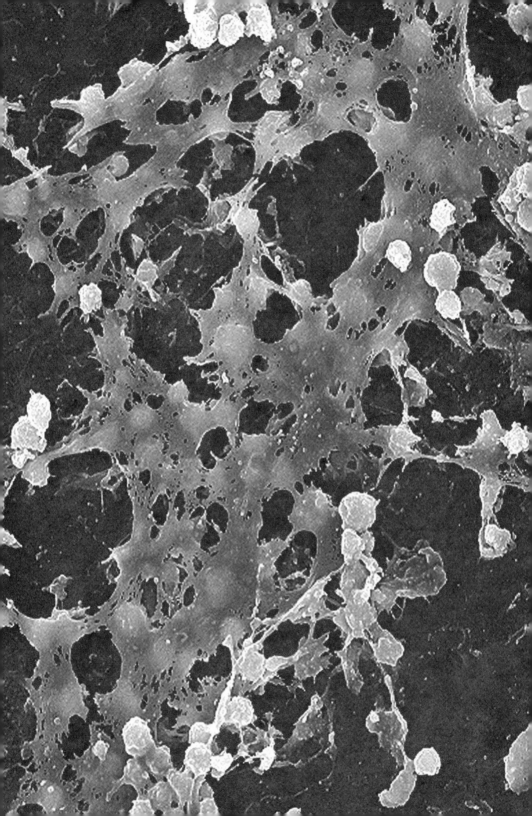

Alas the internet ~~is winning~~
                    has no body in the infinite ~~margin~~
                                    ~~capability~~
                              torrent

& tumbles like fruit that has ~~rotted on the tree~~
                        passed from ~~bud to ash~~
                                  a cold intelligence

          into ~~my hand~~
               the hand in my ~~imagination~~
                       online persona ~~of myself~~

❧

One must have a ~~mind of winter~~
                body of information

            ~~at one's fingertips~~
            ~~on one's plate~~
            before one's incorporeal consciousness can blossom

like ~~a cybernetic flower~~
        the ~~idea of a cybernetic flower~~
                archived record of the idea of a cybernetic flower

                which will make its patent holder wealthy

                            ~~beyond her wildest dreams~~
                within the scale of her wildest dreams

❧

~~She will sit in the electric current of the false sun~~
~~She will sit under the glare of its eye~~
She will have a mole on her cheek in the shape of a three-headed dog

❧

Even as metadata I want to ~~feel your body beside me~~
                            ~~congregate with other metadata~~
                know what it is to be known ~~biblically~~

& thus do I make myself whole
in the vaults of the Never-ending Sex Act

The law of chaos is the law ~~of ideas~~
which cannot be uprooted

by anything other than ~~geometry~~
the organization of ~~synaptic terminals~~
~~syntactical adjuncts~~
~~declarative clauses~~
proteins

into strands of amino acids

When ~~I am collected~~
~~the information in my e-mail is collected~~
even my ~~unthinking~~ cells are collected

let us sit together ~~again~~ beside the river
& gather the leaves as they pass

~~& our hands will dip into the pulp~~
& the watchers will hear for a moment the garbled

choking of the current

& together we will ~~slow-dissolve into eternity~~
join the unsexed ancients

in the ~~invisible~~ room that exists outside of time

Here we both sit ~~naked but for the weight of our bodies~~
　　　　　　~~gathering invisible leaves~~
　　　　　　~~gazing into the coded rectangular window~~
　　　　　　~~the page between us a skin~~
　　　　　　~~the skin between us a film~~
　　　　　　~~the film on pause but somehow moving~~
　　　　　　having the same thought ~~at the same time~~

　　& in the other room ~~Heather~~
　　　　　　　my wife ~~is asleep~~
　　　　　　　　　is most awake & active & lives

　　　her life beyond the margins of my limited imagination

Oh I said listening to ~~*the raucous words of the nightclouds*~~
　　　　　the quietness of ~~breath~~
　　　　　　　　the wind
　　　　With ~~my hand~~
　　　　　the invisible hand

　　　　I touch her face softly ~~so as not to wake her~~

　　　　　& both our breaths quicken

　I will not ~~take part in any form of ownership~~
　　　　adhere to the patrilineal subjugation of women

　　　　　　　She is not my vehicle

　　　　This is a matrimonial revision

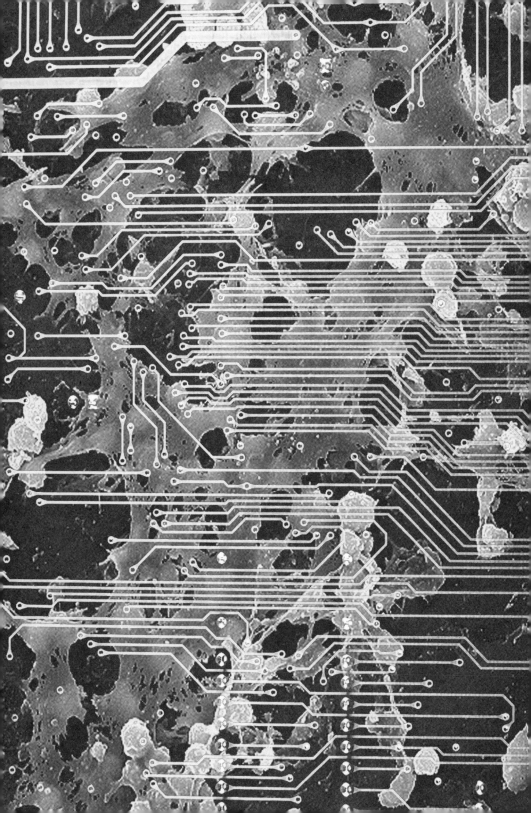

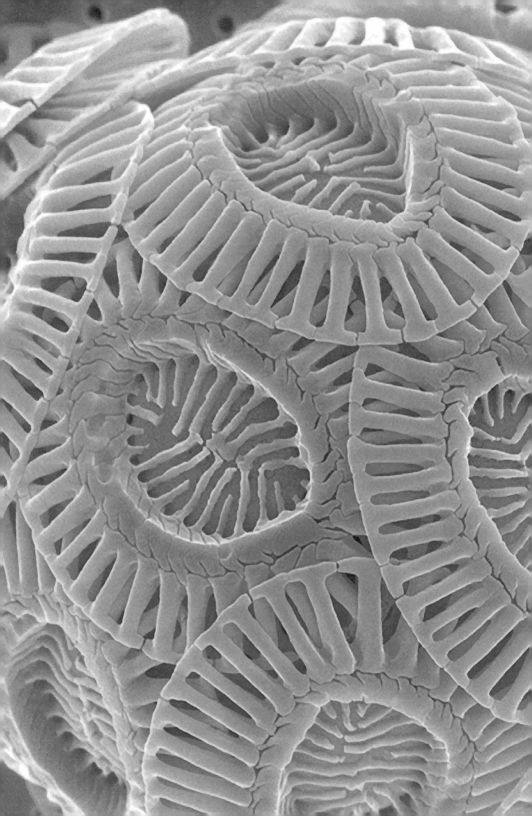

I have ~~broken through the membrane~~
      beheld a kingdom built of ~~math~~
                geometric ~~figures~~
                     fractals

in the bath
I combed my hair & immediately wet it again

      ~~I want to tell you~~ how good it felt

❧

I am not in hysterics the ~~stained glass sky~~
                    emperor ~~of ice cream~~
                          moth

        is the king of ~~nothing its~~ eyes ~~apprehend~~
                                    ~~are not its eyes~~
                                painted on like zeros

        & can teach humanity ~~the foul compote~~
                            to spread on toast like jam

                the paste of ~~dusty-winged euphoria~~
                            immediate & absolute awareness

❧

I am ~~inconsolable~~
        inconsolably convinced

                    that *we ourselves belong to* ~~*the sea*~~
                                    ~~the jungle~~
                                    pure ~~information~~

        & swim like waterbugs chewed up ~~with visions~~
                                by ~~Amazonian fish~~
                                    ~~living plants~~
                                    ~~Nepenthes~~
                                    ~~the California pitcher plant~~
                                    ~~sundews~~
                                    venus fly traps

                which close like mouths around their prey

34

Asleep on the subway I dream of ~~graboids~~
~~crocodiles~~
the lens & cornea

of the pineal gland in reptiles

What does the moth see through ~~its wings~~
the eyes on its wings

& why ~~does the insect's mouth fuse in adulthood~~
is the only letter missing
between moth & mouth
~~the U~~
the grinning mouth of letters

The great third-eyed crocodiles

~~alseep in their dens~~
invade the dens of ~~otters~~
~~beavers~~
toads that croak & croak at night

~~Where are our ponds~~
~~We must create more complex ponds~~
The city ~~has no lotus blossoms~~
itself is a living ~~body of water~~
membrane through which ~~we pass~~
to launch

into the Diaphanous ~~Metaphysical Translation~~
Machinations of ~~Transport~~
Time-space

A ~~mere whiff of smoke~~

~~The~~ whole world

becomes itself ~~invisible~~ in the mist

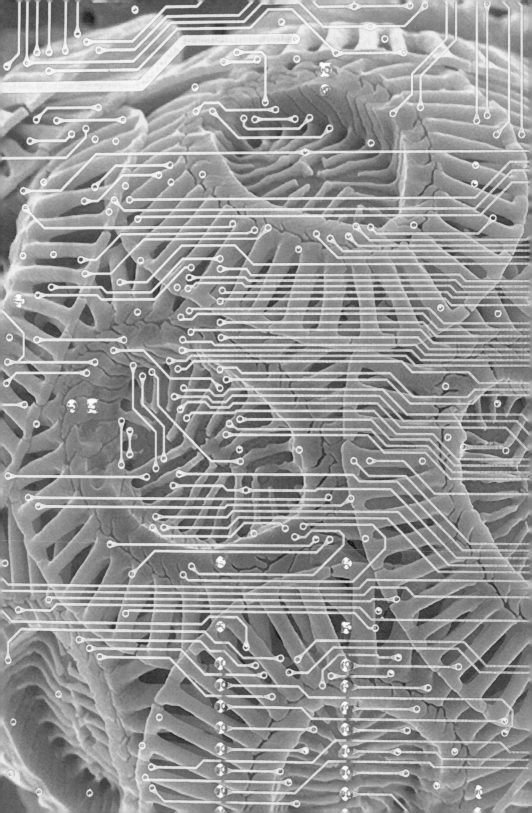

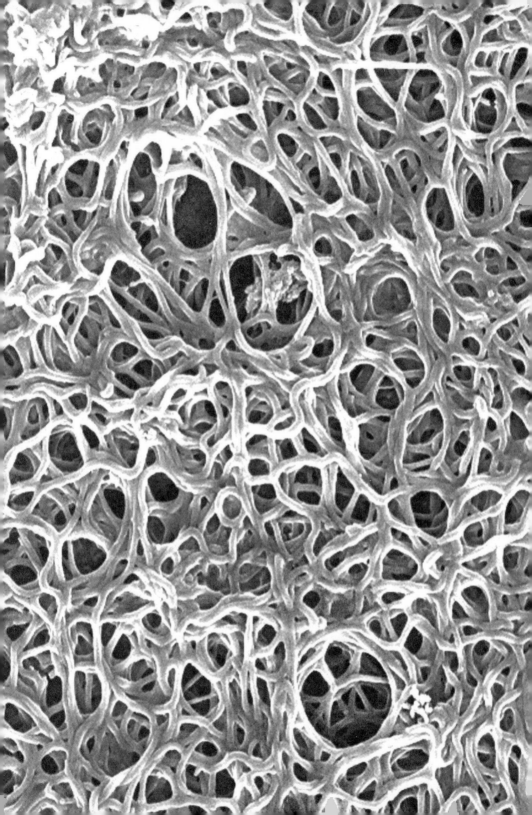

In kitchen cups ~~concupiscent curds~~
        a minuscule strand of *~~cogito~~ ergot ~~sum~~*

           snaked into the mind of ~~the son of a toolmaker~~
                                ~~a late-working chemist~~
                                an accidental scholar
                                        of boundlessness

who bicycled home & vanished ~~his ego~~ into the Swiss countryside

I fell asleep and awoke the next morning ~~feeling perfectly well~~
having instantaneously

~~transmuted consciousness~~
~~restructured the architecture of his mind~~
salvaged the wreckage of ~~humanity~~
a single college student

who was myself

lying prone & susceptible in the grass

dozens of years later ~~exhausted of reason~~
grappling with forces locked inside the body

&

The ~~unbroken~~ narrative of Western philosophy is ~~a lie~~
predicated

on the false claim

that ~~body is separate from psyche~~
~~subject is not object~~
~~*thought and the object of thought are the same*~~
a thing can be ~~halved~~ by speaking its name

Consider this the great joke!

♠

~~Outside my window the sun speaks itself alight~~
~~I say the word *raindrop* and know it will rain~~
The breath of words freezes & falls in the air as moisture

In the shaman's creation myth of the ~~future~~
~~devastation~~
inevitably changing multiverse

Trickster is played by ~~Coyote~~
~~a Photoshopped image of Coyote~~
the entire internet filled with cats

♠

~~The bit of apple in the bowl of soap that kills the flies~~
~~The emperor moth that lands on the general's shoulder~~
The chemical compounds which are seen first in sleep

~~as saw the organic chemist Kekulé~~
~~the structure of Benzene in a dream of Ouroboros~~

unlock the ~~oscillating dual nature of matter~~
eventual recognition ~~of nonlocality~~
that a molecule

can have alternating single and double bonds between atoms

& thus begins the era of ~~petrochemical engineering~~
~~plastics~~
microbeads in ~~soaps~~
~~rivers~~
every bird & fish's gut

~~Nobody is ever missing~~
nothing is ever finished

but the snake ~~eating its own tail~~

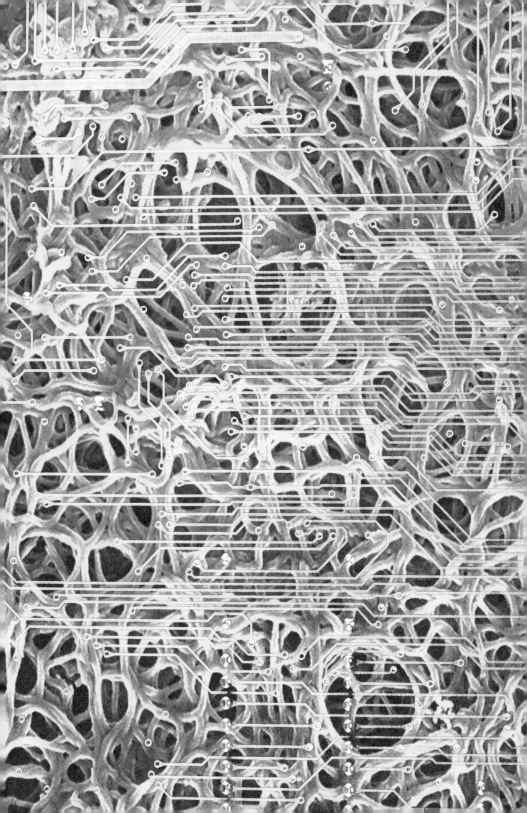

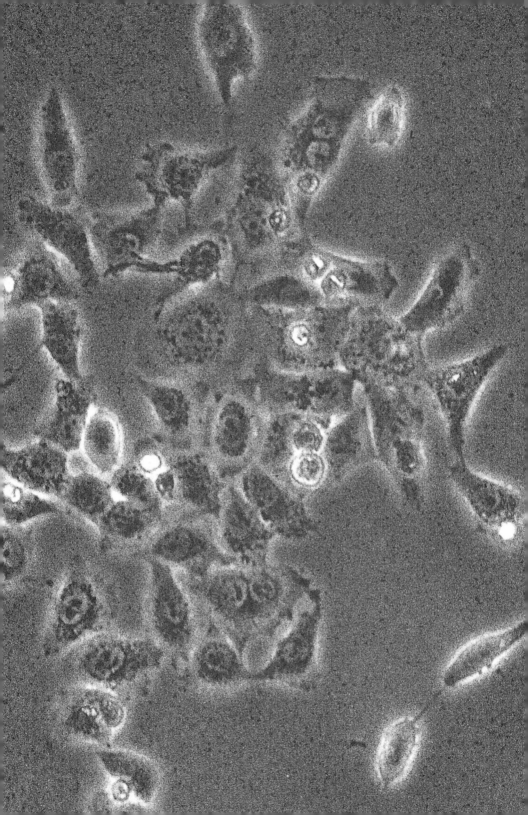

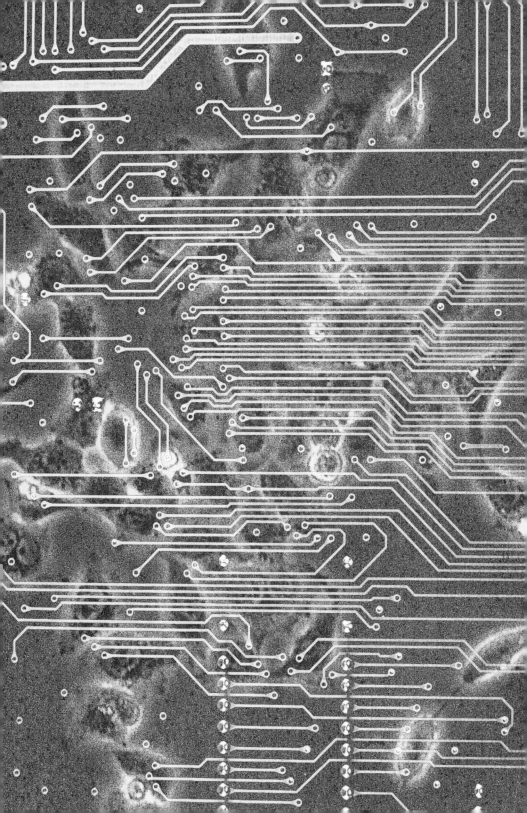

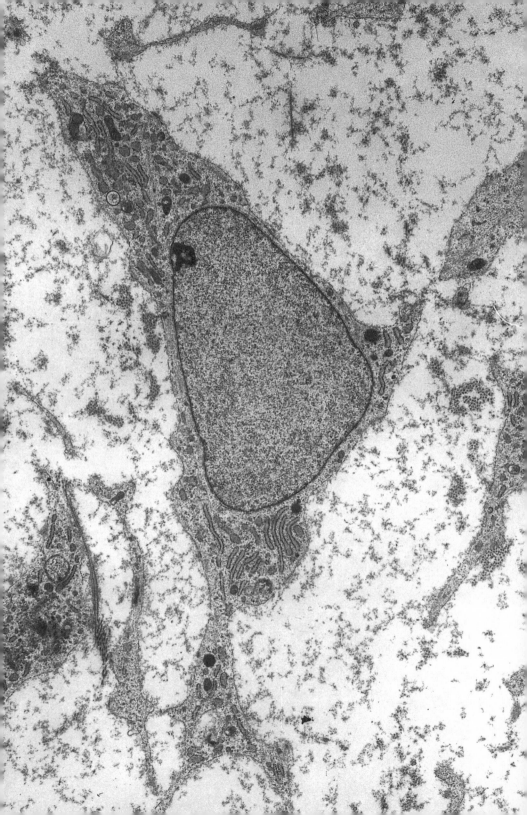

I met a girl ~~online~~
　　　　　　　　~~in the woods outside of time~~
　　　　　　　　somewhere in Brooklyn

　　In the first ~~poem I wrote for her~~
　　　　　　　　darkness around us a cold wind

　　　　　　　　blew from ~~her window~~
　　　　　　　　　　　the machine in her window

　　　　　　~~on both our thighs the gooseflesh raised~~
　　　　　　the temperature fluctuated

as in a percolator continuously filled with ice

What drugs are these ~~the body makes~~
　　　　　　　　our bodies make together

🦋

I wrestled ~~that night~~ with lizards in my sleep

& turned away from ~~her~~
            what I imagined ~~her to be in my dream~~

she kissed my ~~shoulder~~
           innermost structure of dense ~~organism~~
                  organic thought-matter
& together rolled over in ~~bed~~
        the bliss of bodily ~~ownership~~
             ~~refusal of ownership~~
             contact!

      what rhythms ~~we wrote~~
      what grandiose schemas we had

🦋

Even that night I ~~held my hand against her own~~
        could not keep my voice inside my chest

       & spoke
       & speak to this day in my sleep

    in language vast as ~~the earth & more dense~~
        the sunken mind

     of a man in solitary confinement

Posiedon I call upon you from my ~~desk~~
                        position in the toss & scup

                                of eternity

            How am I not to despise ~~myself~~
                        my own ~~silence~~
                                inaction

Last night I ~~sat down to watch a program on Hulu~~
            ~~was confronted by men and their guns~~
            wanted to ~~see just one innocuous nipple~~
                  hear just one ~~nonviolent~~ fuckword

      Instead there was ~~the gratuitous slitting of 3 human throats~~
                        ~~one woman raped & then left in the mud~~
                        ~~a total of sixteen mutilated bodies~~
                        ~~an infinitude of dark-skinned villians~~
                        ~~one hero with a trunk full of guns~~
                        a bus bombing that killed thirteen &
was valorized by the slow-motion beauty of shrapnel moving
through the air like raindrops which emanated all from the blast's
magnificent axis

❧

are your brains drying up is your flesh

drying up ~~the spirits the gods~~ the visions I've seen ~~them~~

& learned ~~from their whispers~~ what language

knows ~~not I know not still~~

❧

yet never did I breathe its pure serene
till I ~~heard Chapman speak out loud~~
   uncovered a bit of old-fashioned music

slipping out from ~~the piece of time I call my own death~~
   beneath the floorboards of my skull

  & eyes! What eyes in the fecund heads of men!

❧

The watcher must ~~watch his own eyes~~
   know of his own distracting gaze

 What is solid ~~can simultaneously exist & not exist~~
   ~~can pass through a solid wall~~
   is comprised mostly of empty space

✎

Consider the effort it costs to ~~eat breakfast~~
 ~~play hockey~~
 take part in the infinite

 ~~permutations of matter~~
 implications of inhabiting

a body & ~~taking it into the street~~
 putting food in the ~~mouth-hole~~
 stomach that ~~goes on forever~~
 for the samurai

unspooled into a fleshy chord which ~~he held in his hands~~
 must have smelled terrible

 all that bile

 as he honored his lord

✎

~~I refuse to believe~~ we are part of a global experiment

Think of the ~~boundless wisdom~~
 ~~esoteric scripture~~
 information contained

 in one ~~computer chip~~
 ~~grain of light~~
 microsecond of lovemaking

Man does not find his way back to the village

    The village is not webbed in electricity

Electricity is not the cause of suffering

    Suffering does not derive from circularity

Circularity provides neither head nor tail

    Without head or tail man is prone to distraction

Distraction strikes not at the yolk of man

    Man does not find his way back to the village

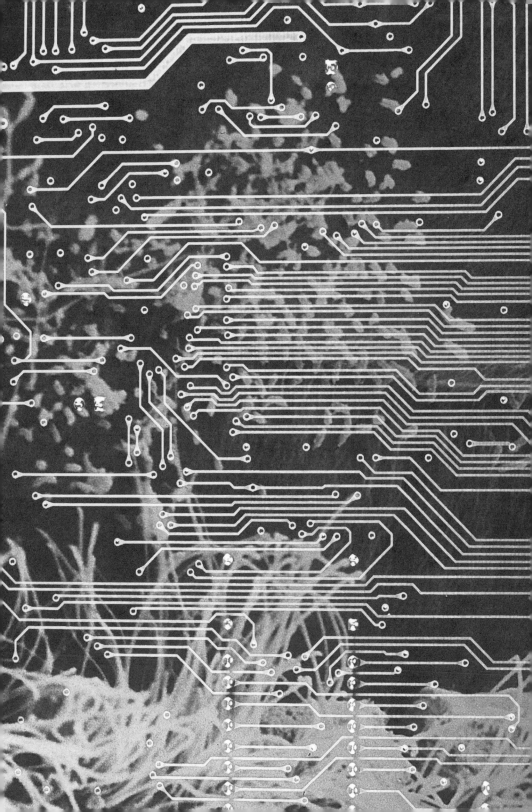

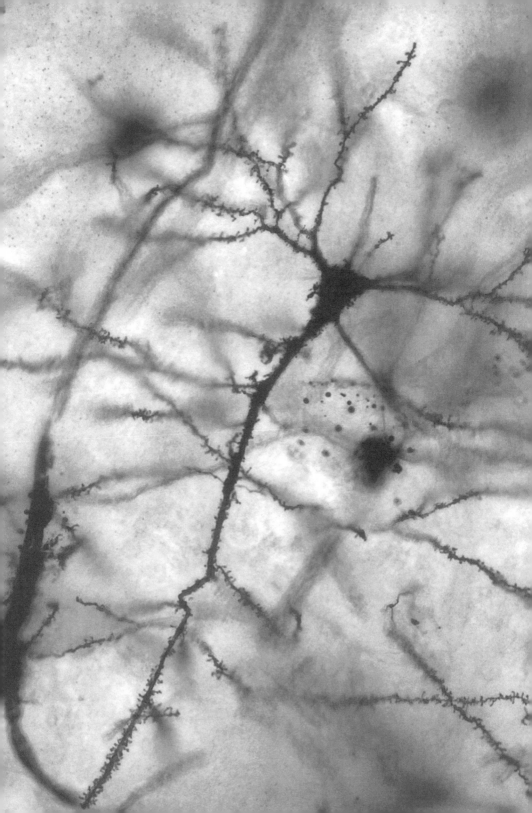

Today in the street I met by chance an old friend from Japan

~~He was delighted to see me~~

We ~~embraced & became ethereal beings~~
    decided to meet at the Stag's Head for drinks

that we might ~~get sozzled~~
             ~~inhibit the glutamate in our brains~~
             ~~become ensorcelled with dopamine~~
             ~~play a round or two of darts~~
             reaffirm our peripherally friendly relationship

                    by becoming ~~the~~ human ~~equivalent of reptiles~~

❦

~~Man knows not what he does~~

Just yesterday I ~~read in the newspaper~~
              ~~scanned on the internet~~
          was in ~~direct receptive~~ communication

with an astrophysicist I have ~~never met~~
                   ~~wanted to become~~
              had the opportunity to entertain

        ~~at an unofficial gathering of scientists~~
        within the gauntlet of my own imagination

❦

In the woods I ~~skinned a bunny~~
             ~~did not skin a bunny~~
          saw a bunny with my own two eyes & pointed out

    Look!

❦

There is a galactic ocean of water in space 12 billion years old
with 140 trillion times all the water on earth

It exists ~~beyond our knowledge of its existence~~
        as mist

◣

Is ~~300 trillion times less dense than our own atmosphere~~
   comprised entirely of water molecules

       fused by ~~pure energy~~
           the residual dynamism of ~~a black hole~~
               what I imagine to be

                the consciousness of plants
                which *flash & yearn*

◣

     We ourselves ~~flash & yearn~~
        are born of this ~~galactic ocean~~
           unfathomably dilute Neopoxy

◣

Our lungs explode like ~~lemons into the glass~~
         pregnant fish ~~pulled by whirlwinds from the sea~~
              ~~raining on the streets~~
            pushed from underground rivers

in the town of Yoro in Honduras

      ~~sometimes twice a year~~ *la Lluvia de Peces*

        deposits small ~~still-living~~ fish

    unknown to the region

first a dark cloud in the sky
a handful of hours of rain

Hundreds of skylarking fish on the ground to take home & eat

the mystifying food

of the gods

To be listless

To be an ocean of fog in the universe

To move lavishly through space
                    as the tongue does in the mouths of dogs

        & human lips!

What incoherently durable modes of transportation
        black & white agency in the sky
                    photographs by Man Ray

        Not the woman's mellifluous back
                (though that as well)
        but the nude on the beach with bulbous metal chess pieces

~~I was with her again last night~~
She had me in ~~spades~~
        all of the ancient positions

        I am over-brimming with magnanimous health

~~I lied on my application~~
~~There was never a ghost on the roof~~
All roofs have been transformed
        by America's most ~~recent economic downgrade~~
                ~~wanted renegades~~
                beautiful retrograde

    motion born to hail the new religion

        of the ~~dismantling of precise & rhetorical observation~~
        accumulation of trinkets

~~to be worn about the neck & shoulders like great Roman hats~~
~~to indicate a very human victory over the flesh~~
to make electric the ancient bath

        as with the initial spark of ~~biopoiesis~~
                ~~abiogenesis~~
                ~~mitosis~~
                life on earth

    given to us by our space overlords
            who ~~do not~~ exist

＊

& still how nice to be wanted even ~~as metadata~~
                            at the behest of men

whose guns about their hips & chests ~~do make us fearfully grin~~
                            they hold like mums

    to be handed out on the eve of the great uprooting

＊

I am an unknowing barbarian

I ~~still haven't returned my library books~~
    am in love with ~~the probability that language is~~ a kind of magic

        & those who spoke the first words were splitting ~~atoms~~
                                            ~~dimensions~~
                                            ~~infinitives~~
                                            hairs

        on some abundant & ungendered god

＊

Do we not have ~~magic in our chests & arms~~
                consciousness even in the tips
                            of our ~~fingers~~
                                plebeian organs

All this flesh & no understanding of the network of organic circuitry

        ~~I am aware of the dearth in this poem~~
        The love story is not a story of conquest

At some point after my birth

I awoke & the sky was replaced with ~~a particulate and intelligent mist~~
a unique & obligatory longing

for more sky

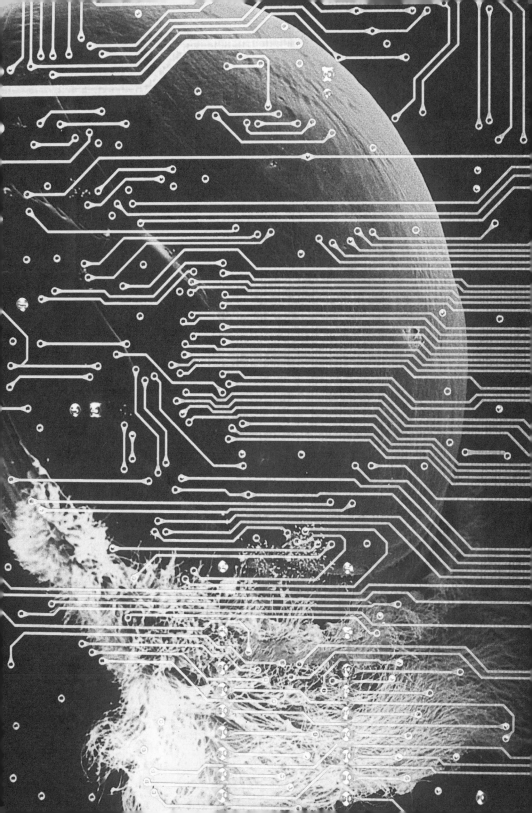

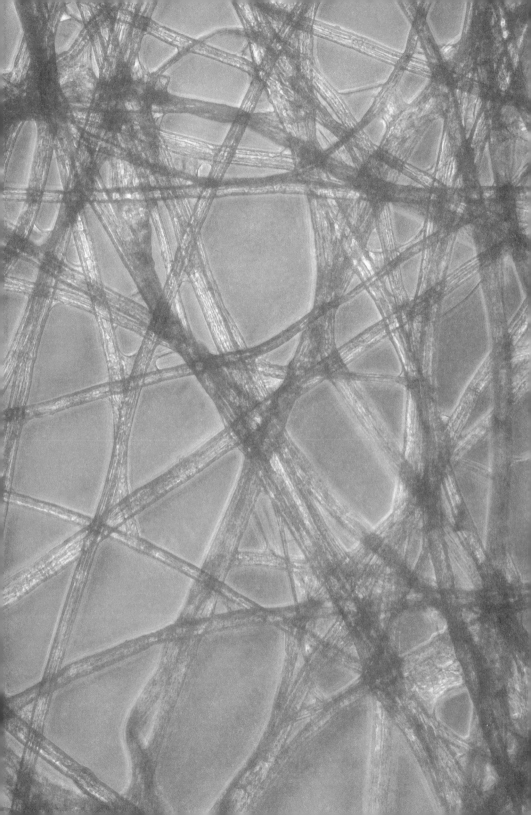

~~I give up the search~~
    ~~I remember my own birth~~
        ~~I know what I know~~

I yam what I yam
ack ack ack ack ack

The sounds of ~~laughter~~
    gunfire even on weekends sometimes

in ~~Baghdad~~
  Brooklyn one ~~is uncertain~~
        feels the presence ~~of the absence~~
            of microchips ~~in the air~~
                in one's

    very own ~~body~~
        dating profile on OKCupid

You are the ~~hottest one for years of night~~
                    singing & the song of dislocation

What I am driving at really

            is that I would like never to sleep alone again

To be eternally awake & substantial
in the presence of a woman

                    ~~I met in the ether~~
                    ~~I love more than all the feathers on all the ducks~~
                    whose very breath is my only hope for air

I chance to live & die ~~a heathen~~
                        in the considerable service of unconditional love

            The whole world became my ~~garden!~~
                            reminder

        that ~~when~~ a thing ~~is wrought that thing~~ is not the self

                    though the self may be lost inside it

        In the garden Heather ~~digs & is attentive to the soil~~
                            ~~is aware of herself as maker & tender~~
                            ~~scatters seeds~~
                            sprays the leaves with oil

❧

I am in detached & prodigious love with the idea of smart-dust
which hankers to prevail upon nature its own necessity

by existing as a fine layer of ~~microelectromechanical systems~~
self-aware & communicative grit

over every ~~single godforsaken~~ thing

including ~~the roads from which it will pilot our vehicles~~
~~the trees which it will light up phosphorescently~~
~~the oceans in which it will teach our fish to speak~~
the air which will become an unfathomably dilute Neopoxy

& our lungs will be filled with ~~microscopic robots~~
biomechanical ~~organisms~~
intelligence

~~not unlike the distribution of Capitalism over all our flesh~~

❧

How selfless is the internet

for ~~delivering the light of awareness to every stinking human~~
teaching humanity the ways & means

of ~~unconditional love~~
mutual destruction

~~with the earth~~
from within the ~~core of the earth~~
sincerity of pop-up advertisements

The reading of thoughts is ~~exceedingly tantalizing~~
                              the act in which you are currently engaged

          here are my thoughts in front of you denatured

Alcohol is ~~mixed with foul smelling compounds & then~~ called *spirits*

      One can ~~open the mind with the addition of substance~~
                distill the nature of a thing by subtraction

                When dark matter collides with matter

          ~~both are expelled from even the confines~~

                              ~~of form & formlessness~~

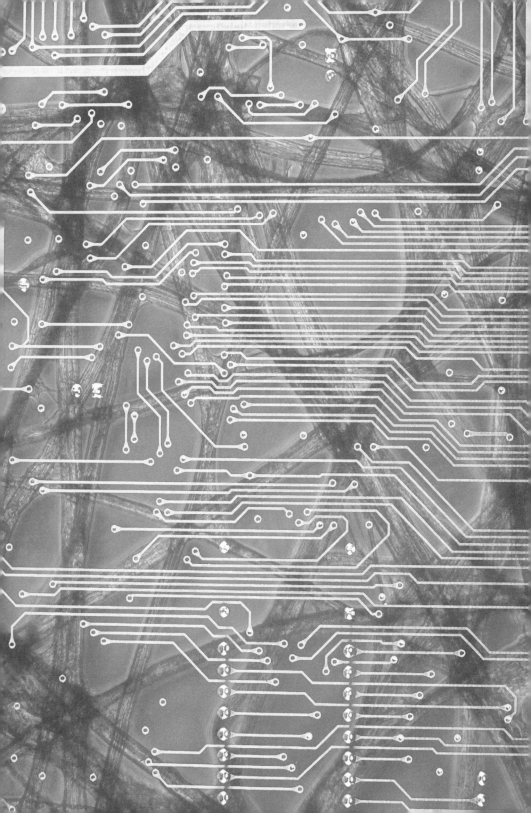

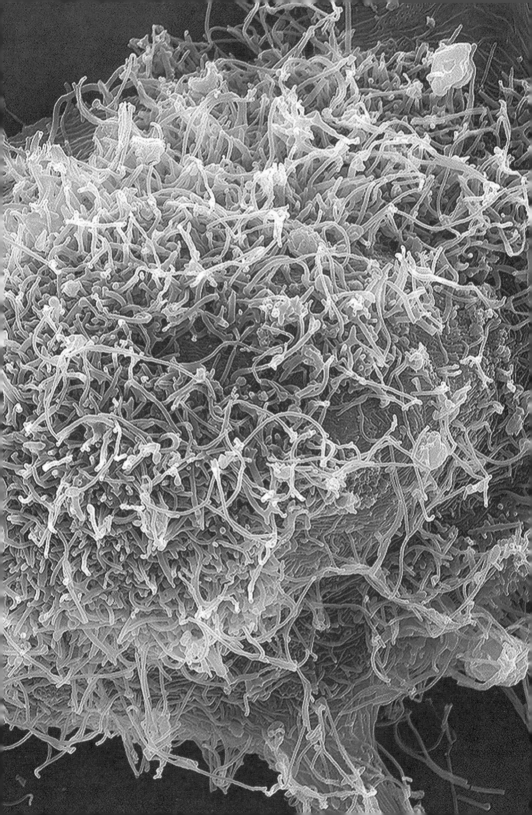

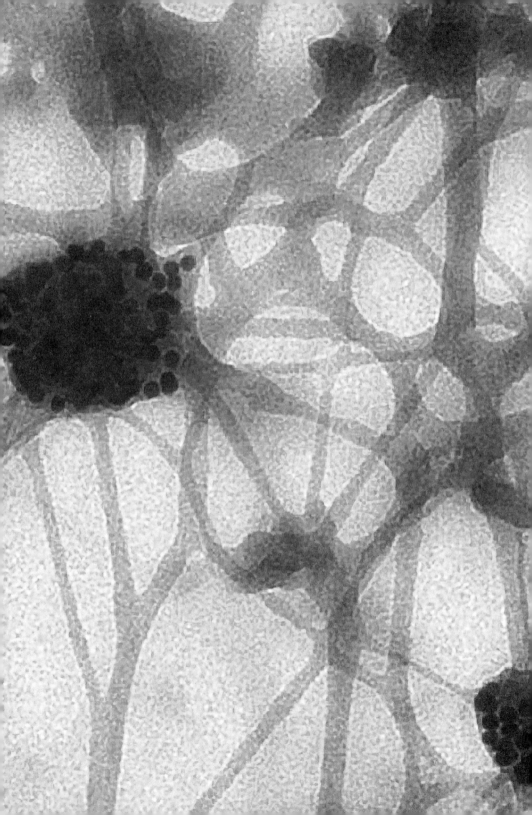

Language itself ~~does not end~~
~~lays down its roots~~
mutates endlessly by means of ~~undoing~~
revision

The mind fills us with wakefulness well before the dawn

Heather in the other room ~~before the child~~
~~full and round as the moon~~
assembling the world

with her mind

that it might suit us all

So many voices ~~here~~ & all of them beyond ~~erasure~~

> ~~Whitman & Stevens~~
> ~~Tennyson & Eliot & Aristotle~~
> ~~Popeye & Longfellow & Hoffman~~
> ~~Berryman & Williams~~
> ~~Keats & Yeats & Ammons~~

> ~~I jostle & burp~~
> ~~I celebrate & irritate myself & my ancestors~~
> ~~I recognize the dearth~~

The canon ~~it shifts like the foot of a wakening giant~~
must reflect the complexity of birth

~~I am the sieve & the cradle~~
~~The earth it breathes behind my eyes~~
There is a soup made of tendrils and vines

> The tendrils are flat as ~~fleas~~
> ~~the legs of a flea~~
> ~~hairs on the legs of a single flea~~

The tendrils are shaped like ~~a spiral staircase~~
braided rope

~~The soup is alive~~

It wants us to know ~~ourselves~~
that something thinking watches

&

Meditating on the peak of a mountain ~~last year~~
                                                                    years ago

I held ~~all the universe inside~~ my skull

                    & promptly lost it again

~~Shadows grow long on liquid & solid alike~~
Even in fog darkness seeds from every particle of light

&

I lean & loafe at my ease observing ~~a spear of summer grass~~
                                        an image of summer grass on Facebook

my eyes ~~twitch & waver across the screen~~
            migrate toward the great & infinite ~~plains~~
                                                ~~pages~~
                                                ~~internet~~
                                                incorporeal mind

                that is ~~the body of~~ the internet

I'm not dead yet
          says the man who is ~~dead~~
                    hard at work

          ~~rewriting his own tenuous grasp on the world~~
          ~~dismantling all the old linear models~~
          peeling an infinitely deep bucket of onions

I grow old ... I grow old ...
I shall ~~*wear the bottoms of my trousers rolled*~~
          cultivate the consciousness of mold

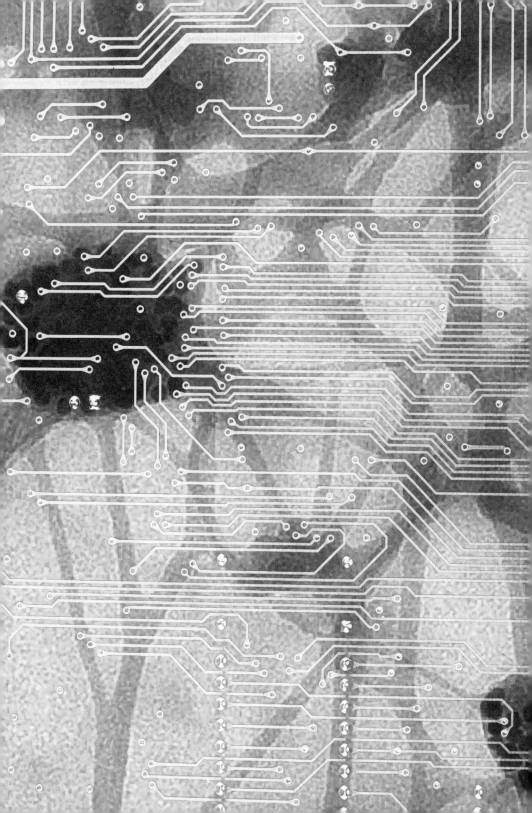

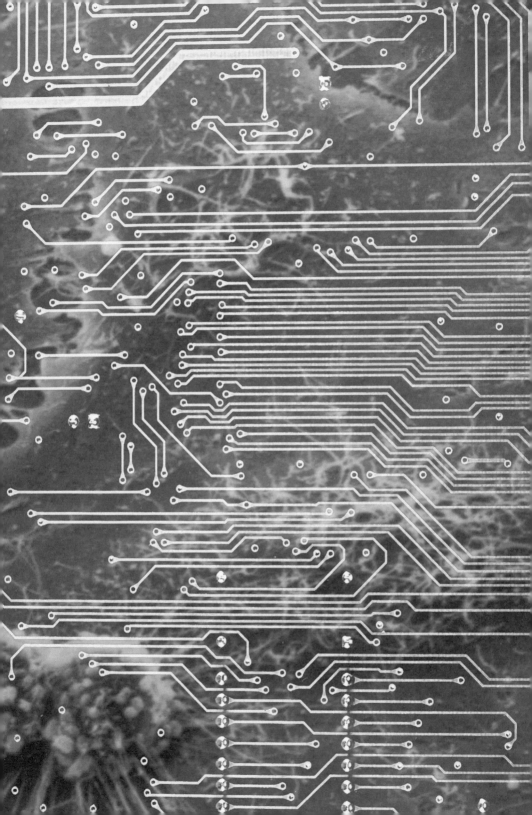

NOTES | ACKNOWLEDGEMENTS

Thanks to AB Gorham at *Black Warrior Review* for devoting space in issue 38.2 to an excerpt of this poem titled "Or Both. We Could Do Both." Your enthusiasm for the project at that early stage was crucial. And to Danniel Schoonebeek at *The Fanzine* for publishing the section that begins "Poseidon I call upon you from my desk."

This is a book of many voices. Beyond those whose words have been written into the text, *Residuum* takes cues and inspiration from the works of Jeremy Narby, Brenda Hillman, Daniel Pinchbeck, Timothy Morton, Alice Notley, C.D. Wright, Forrest Gander, and countless other ecological thinkers.

With the exception of one, the interstitial images used to delineate sections are scanning electron micrographs and range in their subjects from viruses to strands of DNA to plant matter to human cells. Further information about individual images available on the last page of this book.

To my ever-growing community of poets & artists & friends, you have taught me what it means to be awake in the world: Craig Rubadoux, Traci Brimhall, Adrienne Perry, Brian Trimboli, Garrett Burrell, Matt Salesess, Phil Ischy, Todd Overby, Robin Coste Lewis, Cathy Che, Bianca Stone, Solmaz Sharif, Elsbeth Pancrazi, Adrian Matejka, Heather Christle, Austin Lagrone, Joe Pan, Glenn Shaheen, Cindy King, Karl Zuehlke, Carlos Hernandez, Allyson Boggess, Ron Villanueva, Jonathan Wells, Zach Martin, Matvei Yanklevich, DTM, Cecilia Llompart, BJ Love, Dan Rosenberg, Jay Deshpande, Jason Koo, Daniel Schoonebeek, Melissa Broder, Luke Davin, Willard Cook, Rich Levy, Misty Matin, Alison DeLima Greene, Bernard Bonnet, Karl Killian, Idra Novey, Conor Bracken, Tricia Taaca, Emily Bludworth de Barrios, Melanie Brkich, Laura Eve Engel, Jacqueline Suskin, and J Vetter in yr yellow hat.

To early readers of the manuscript, you live in this book. Thank you for lending your complex brains, your music, and your experience to the project: Henk Rossouw, Karyna McGlynn, Erika Jo Brown, Luisa Muryadan, Monica Wendel, Chris Murray, Georgia Pearle, Paul Hlava, Chris Hutchinson, Katie Condon, Nathan Stabenfeldt, Meghan Martin, and most of all my teachers Nick Flynn, Ilya Kaminsky, J Kastely, Tony Hoagland, Kevin Prufer, & Roberto Tejada. *Residuum* would not be what it is without you.

To my editor Caryl Pagel, thank you for your encouragement, your vision, your time, your patience, & your guidance. I wish for every writer the experience of working with an editor as intelligent and devoted as you and the entire staff at Cleveland State University Poetry Center.

I've had the good fortune to learn from so many of my poetry heroes. To leave them out would be to ignore those forces that have shaped me. In addition to those mentioned above, I am forever indebted to Erin Belieu, Breyton Breytonbach, Martha Collins, Ginny Grimsley, Kimiko Hahn, Edward Hirsch, Jen Hofer, Major Jackson, James Kimbrell, David Kirby, Yusef Komunyakkaa, Deborah Landau, Dana Levin, Sharon Olds, Martha Serpas, Charles Simic, Michael Snediker, & Matthew Rohrer.

For their support and for giving me the time and space to write, I am grateful to the New York University Creative Writing Program, the Starworks Foundation, St. Mary's Hospital, the University of Houston Creative Writing Program, Centrum's Port Townsend Writers Conference, Mt. Tremper Arts, InPrint Houston, Writers in the Schools (WITS), Texas Children's Hospital, the Museum of Fine Arts Houston, & the Florida State University Creative Writing Program.

To my family and families, I am your poet. To my parents, Andrew, Elli, Mike, Nancy, thank you for teaching me to love the world, and for giving me something to write about. And to my wife Heather, all of it is for you.

Tom, you were the best of all of us. Humanity is less graceful without you.

A NOTE ON THE TYPE

Baskerville was designed in England in 1754 by master type-founder and printer John Baskerville. Though the typeface did not gain notoriety in its creator's lifetime, it made its way to France and Italy and eventually influenced the development of modern faces such as Didot and Bodoni. In 1917, American typographer Bruce Rogers discovered a Baskerville type specimen in a Cambridge bookstore and recast the type, reviving the font in the 20th century.

Interior designed and typset by Martin Rock.